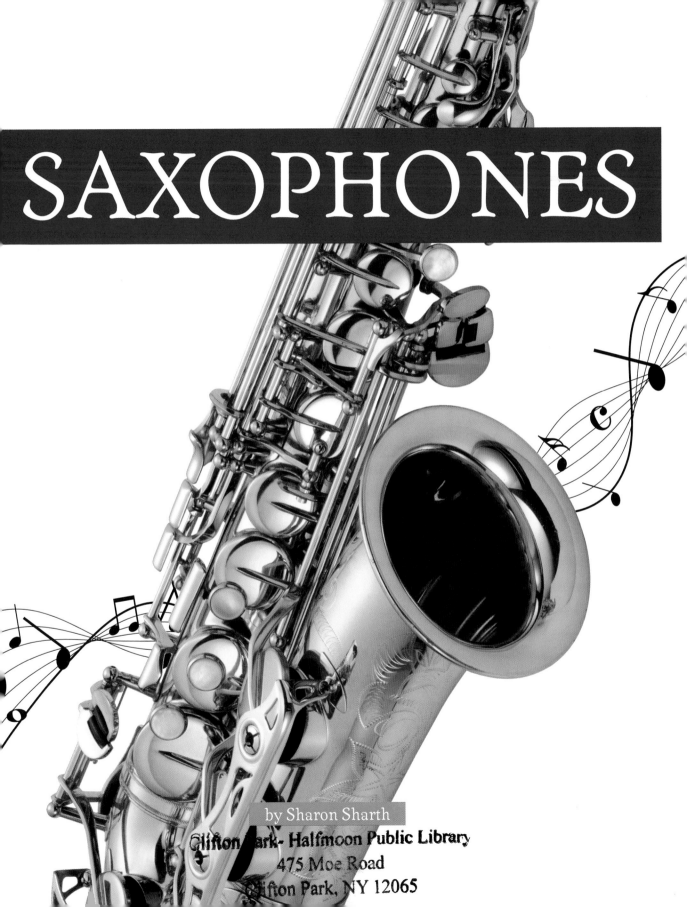

SAXOPHONES

by Sharon Sharth

Published by The Child's World®
1980 Lookout Drive • Mankato, MN 56003-1705
800-599-READ • www.childsworld.com

Design element: Vector memory/Shutterstock.com
Photo credits: Africa Studio/Shutterstock.com: 18; Alenavlad/Shutterstock.com: 21 (oboe); Andrea Nissotti/
Shutterstock.com: 21 (flute); Andrey_Popov/Shutterstock.com: 21 (clarinet); Aspen Photo/Shutterstock.com:
4; Axel Alvarez/Shutterstock.com: 11; Boris Medvedev/Shutterstock.com: 8 (tenor, alto, and baritone), 21
(piccolo); Donna Ellen Coleman/Shutterstock.com: 17; furtseff/Shutterstock.com: 21 (bassoon); horiyan/
Shutterstock.com: cover, 1; moonfish8/Shutterstock.com: 8 (soprano); mphot/Shutterstock.com: 12; Mr
Twister/Shutterstock.com: 14; SFC/Shutterstock.com: 7; Wilawan Khasawong/123RF: 21 (recorder)

ISBN: 9781503831926
LCCN: 2018960557

Printed in the United States of America
PA02417

Table *of* Contents

CHAPTER ONE

The Saxophone

You hear its joyful cry at football games when the marching band strolls by. You hear it wail in jazz bands and growl on television and in films. What instrument is almost as expressive as the human voice? It's the saxophone!

❮ *This woman is playing a saxophone at a football game.*

CHAPTER TWO

What Is a Saxophone?

A saxophone is a musical instrument made of metal, usually brass. It is part of a group of instruments called **woodwinds**. Woodwind instruments make sound when you blow air through

Former U.S. President Bill Clinton plays the saxophone.

them. You can make different sounds by covering or opening the holes on the tube, or body, of the instrument. Oboes and flutes are woodwinds, too.

It takes a lot of air to play a saxophone. ❯

soprano
saxophone

baritone
saxophone

alto
saxophone

tenor
saxophone

8

CHAPTER THREE

Different Kinds of Saxophones

The saxophone, or "sax," was invented more than 170 years ago by Adolphe Sax, a Belgian instrument maker. Saxophones come in different sizes. The bass saxophone is the largest and plays the lowest sounds, or **notes**. The highest notes come from the smallest sax, the soprano saxophone. Between these two are alto, tenor, and baritone saxophones. The alto and tenor are the most popular saxophones to play.

❮ *Here you can see some of the different kinds of saxophones.*

CHAPTER FOUR

What Shape are Saxophones?

A saxophone is shaped a little like a letter J. Besides a saxophone's tube-like body, it has a **mouthpiece** at one end. The other end curves upward and is shaped like a bell. Saxophones with a longer body can play lower notes. Saxophones with a shorter body can play higher notes. That is why baritone and soprano saxophones sound so different!

Soprano saxophones also have a different shape. Their straight body makes them look something like a clarinet.

You can sit or stand up to play a saxophone. ❯

CHAPTER FIVE

The Mouthpiece

To play a saxophone, you blow air through the mouthpiece. A single, flat **reed** is attached to the mouthpiece. The reed makes a sound as it **vibrates**, or moves back and forth, against the mouthpiece.

The mouthpiece for some beginner saxophones are made of plastic.

   To make the right kind of sounds, you must blow directly into the mouthpiece. Don't let the air escape! You must also make sure the reed is moist. If it is dry, it can't vibrate, and the sax will squeak.

❮ *Players keep the reed wet by licking it.*

CHAPTER SIX

The Keys

The saxophone's tube-like body has 20 holes. A small, padded flap covers each hole when you press a button, or **key**. When most of the holes are open, the saxophone can play higher notes. Closing more holes produces lower notes.

A saxophone's keys are sometimes called "pad cups."

❮ *The flaps can sometimes make a soft clicking sound.*

CHAPTER SEVEN

Playing the Saxophone

To play a saxophone, you hold it in front of you with your fingers resting lightly on the keys. Then you blow air into the mouthpiece to make the reed vibrate. The air moves through the body of the sax. You push the keys to open and close the holes. Opening and closing the holes changes where the air can come out. That determines how high or low the notes will be.

A person who plays a saxophone is called a saxophonist.

Some saxophones have a neck strap the player can wear. ❯

CHAPTER EIGHT

Jazz Saxophone

The saxophone is popular in jazz music. One of the most famous American jazz saxophone players was Charlie Parker. His nickname was "Bird," and he could make his saxophone sing like one. He played the alto sax and helped create a new style of music called bebop. Bebop music is based on making up sounds, or **improvising**, in front of the audience.

❮ *John Coltrane, Sonny Rollins, and Stan Getz are all famous jazz saxophonists.*

A saxophone can make many of the same sounds you can make with your voice. It can sing, laugh, and even scream! A saxophone can sound brassy and loud. It can sound soothing and gentle. You can play pop, jazz, and classical music on a sax. Would you like to play the saxophone?

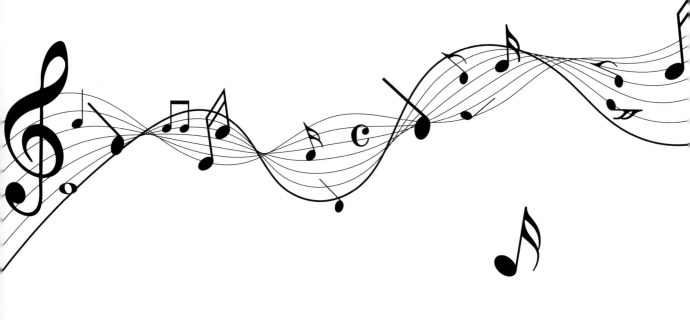

Other Woodwind Instruments

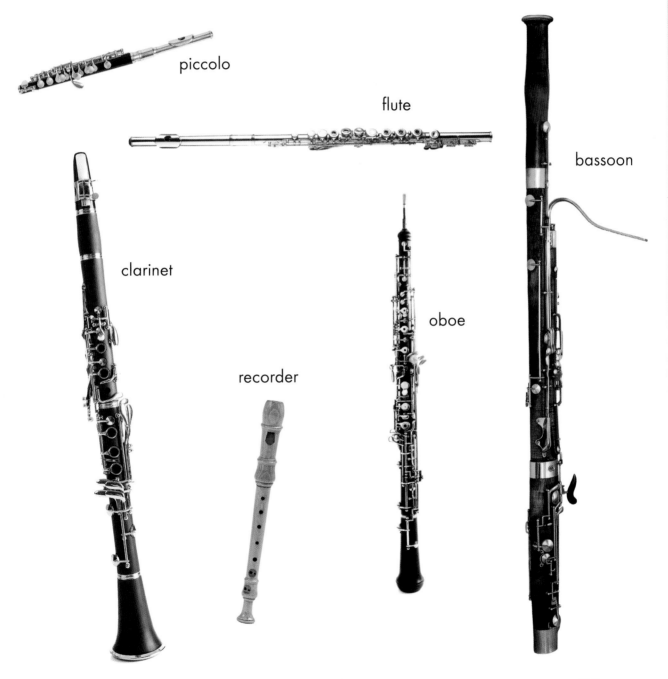

piccolo

flute

bassoon

clarinet

oboe

recorder

Glossary

improvising (IM-pruh-vy-zing) Improvising is making something up as you go along. Improvising is a big part of some kinds of jazz music, such as bebop.

key (KEEZ) On a saxophone, keys are small buttons you press to cover holes along the saxophone's body.

mouthpiece (MOWTH-peece) The mouthpiece is the part of an instrument where you place your mouth to play. Blowing air through the mouthpiece produces sound.

notes (NOHTS) A note is a musical sound. Pressing the keys on a saxophone produces different notes.

reed (REED) On some instruments, including saxophones, a reed is a thin piece of wood, metal, or plastic fastened to the mouthpiece. Blowing air into the mouthpiece moves the reed and makes a sound.

vibrates (VY-brayt) When something vibrates, it moves back and forth very quickly. Blowing into a saxophone mouthpiece makes the reed vibrate against the mouthpiece.

woodwinds (WOOD-windz) Woodwinds are tube-shaped musical instruments that you play by blowing air through them. Saxophones are woodwinds.

To Learn More

IN THE LIBRARY

Cline, Thornton. *The Amazing Incredible Shrinking Saxophone.* Anaheim Hills, CA: Centerstream Publishing, 2018.

Landau, Elaine. *Is the Saxophone for You?* Minneapolis, MN: Lerner Publications, 2014.

Nunn, Daniel. *Woodwind.* Chicago, IL: Heinemann Library, 2012.

ON THE WEB

Visit our website for links about saxophones:

childsworld.com/links

Note to Parents, Teachers, and Librarians: We routinely verify our Web links to make sure they are safe and active sites. So encourage your readers to check them out!

Index

About the Author

Sharon Sharth is an actress, playwright, and award-winning author who has written books about everything from animals to countries. Sharon has acted on TV, in films, and on Broadway. She spends much of her time in Los Angeles and New York.